The T♡ddler's handb☺☺k

with over **100 Words**
that every kid should know

BY DAYNA MARTIN

الإنجليزية / العربية

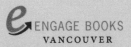

ENGAGE BOOKS

VANCOUVER

1

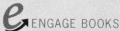 ENGAGE BOOKS

Mailing address
PO BOX 4608
Main Station Terminal
349 West Georgia Street
Vancouver, BC
Canada, V6B 4A1

www.engagebooks.ca

Written & compiled by: Dayna Martin
Edited, designed & translated by: A.R. Roumanis
Proofread by: Reem Mokhtar
Photos supplied by: Shutterstock
Photo on page 47 by: Faye Cornish

FIRST EDITION / FIRST PRINTING

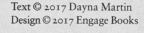

LIBRARY AND ARCHIVES CANADA CATALOGUING IN PUBLICATION

Martin, Dayna, 1983–, author
   The toddler's handbook : numbers, colors, shapes, sizes, ABC animals, opposites, and sounds, with over 100 words that every kid should know / written by Dayna Martin ; edited by A.R. Roumanis.

Issued in print and electronic formats.
Text in English and Arabic.
ISBN 978-1-77226-448-7 (bound). –
ISBN 978-1-77226-449-4 (paperback). –
ISBN 978-1-77226-450-0 (pdf). –
ISBN 978-1-77226-451-7 (epub). –
ISBN 978-1-77226-452-4 (kindle)

1. Arabic language – Vocabulary – Juvenile literature.
2. Vocabulary – Juvenile literature.
3. Word recognition – Juvenile literature.
I. Martin, Dayna, 1983– . Toddler's handbook.
II. Martin, Dayna, 1983– . Toddler's handbook. Arabic.
III. Title.

PJ6166.M37 2017   J492.7'181   C2017-905762-6
                                       C2017-905763-4

الحروف الأبجدية Alhuruf al' abjadia 4 **ABCs**	الأعداد Al' aedad 11 **Numbers**	الألوان Al'alwan 14 **Colors**	الأضداد Al' addad 16 **Opposites**
الأشكال Al'ashkal 22 **Shapes**	الأصوات Al' aswat 24 **Sounds**	الأفعال Al'afeal 28 **Actions**	العواطف Aleawatif 30 **Emotions**
الرياضه Alriyaduh 32 **Sports**	المحركات Almuharikat 34 **Engines**	الأحجام Al'ahjam 36 **Sizes**	الجسم Aljism 38 **Body**
أدوات المائدة 'Adawat almayida 40 **Tableware**	الملابس Almalabis 42 **Clothes**	وقت الاستحمام Waqt alaistihmam 44 **Bath Time**	ميعاد النوم Miyead alnuwm Bed Time 45 3

Aa

تمساح إستوائي

Tamsah 'iistwayiy

Alligator

Bb

دب

Daba

Bear

4

Cc

قطة

Qata

Cat

كلب
Kalb

Dd

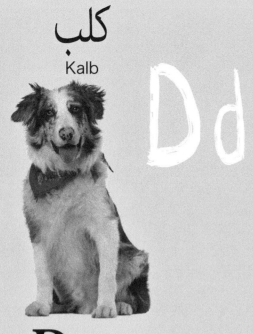

Dog

فيل
Fil

Ee

Elephant

ثعلب
Thaelab

Ff

Fox

معزة
Mueiza

Gg

Goat   5

Hh

حصان
Hisan

Horse

Ii

الإغوانا
Al' iighwana

Iguana

Jj

نمر
Namur

Jaguar

الكوالة

Alkawala

Kk

Koala

أسد

'Asada

Ll

Lion

فأر

Far

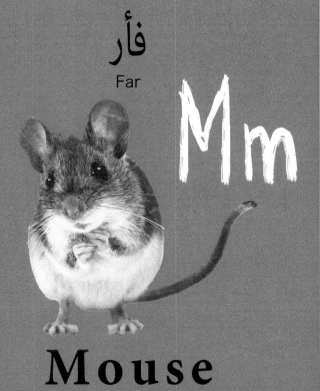

Mm

Mouse

سلمندر

Slmndr

Nn

Newt 7

قندس
Qandus

O o

Otter

خنزير
Khinzir

P p

Pig

السمان
Alsaman

Q q

8 **Quail**

أرنب
'Arnab

R r

Rabbit

كلب البحر
Klb albahr

S s

Seal

نمر
Namur

T t

Tiger

سعدان الواكاري
Suedan alwakary

U u

Uakari

نسر
Nasir

V v

Vulture 9

Ww

Weasel

Xx

X-ray fish

Yy

ثور التبيت

Thawr altabiat

10   **Yak**

Zz

الحمار الوحشي

Alhimar alwahshiu

Zebra

تفاحة

Tafaha

واحد

Wahed

١

1

One

Apple

المقرمشات

Almuqarmashat

اثنين

Ethnein

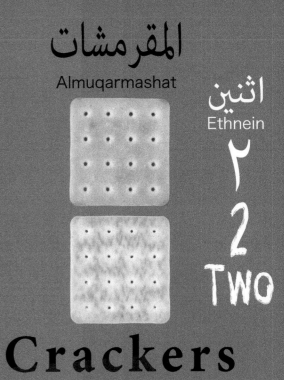

٢

2

Two

Crackers

شرائح البطيخ

Sharayih albatikh

ثلاثة

Thalatha

 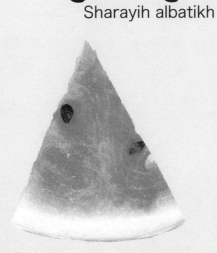 

٣

3

Three

Watermelon slices

11

فراولة

Farawila

أربعة

Arba-a

٤

4

Four

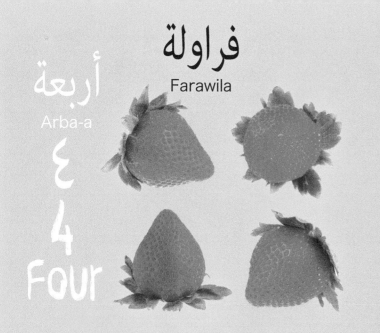

Strawberries

جزر

Juzur

خمسة

Khamsa

٥

5

Five

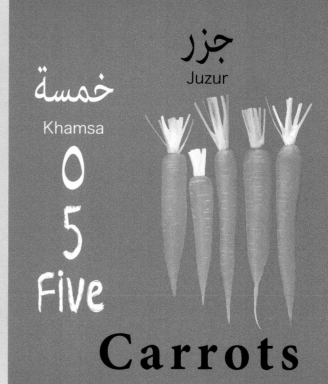

Carrots

طماطم

Tamatim

ستة

Sitta

٦

6

Six

12

Tomatoes

قرع
Qarae

سبعة
Sab-a

٧
7
Seven

Pumpkins

شرائح الفاكهة
Sharayih alfakiha

ثمانية
Thamanya

٨
8
Eight

Fruit slices

بطاطس
Batatis

تسعة
Tis-a

٩
9
Nine

Potatoes

بسكويت
Baskuit

عشرة
Ashara

١٠
10
Ten

Cookies 13

قوس قزح

Qus qazah

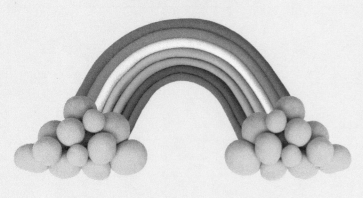

Rainbow

أحمر

'Ahmar

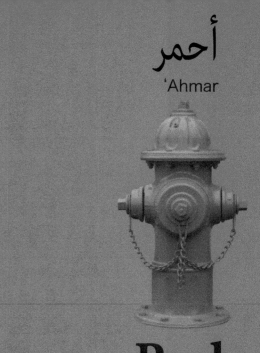

Red

برتقالى

Birtaqalaa

Orange

أصفر

'Asfar

Yellow

أخضر

'Akhdir

Green

أزرق

'Azraq

Blue

اللون النيلي

Allawn alnayliu

Indigo

بنفسجى

Binafsjaa

Violet 15

فوق
Fawq

Up

أسفل
'Asfal

Down

داخل
Dakhil

In

خارج
Kharij

Out

16

ساخن

Sakhin

Hot

بارد

Barid

Cold

مبلل

Mubalal

Wet

جاف

Jaf

Dry

17

أمام
'Amam

Front

خلف
khalf

Back

يشعل
Yusheil

18 **On**

يطفىء
Yatfaa'

Off

مفتوح

Maftuh

Open

مغلق

Mughlaq

Closed

فارغ

Khashab

Empty

ممتلئ

Mumtali

Full

19

آمنة

Amina

Safe

خطير

Khatir

Dangerous

كبير

Sagheer

20 **Big**

صغير

Kabeer

Small

نائم
Nayim

Asleep

مستيقظ
Mustayqiz

Awake

طويل
Tawil

Long

قصير
Qasir

Short 21

دائرة

Dayira

Circle

مربع

Murabae

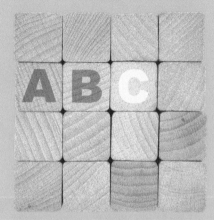

Square

مثلث

Muthalath

22 **Triangle**

مستطيل

Mustatil

Rectangle

معين
Maein

Diamond

نجمة
Najima

Star

بيضوي
Baydwy

Oval

قلب
Qalb

Heart   23

عطس
Eats

اتشووووو
Atashu wawawaw

Ah-choo

Sneeze

بطة
Bata

كواااك
Kawaaaak

Quack

Duck

بقرة
Baqara

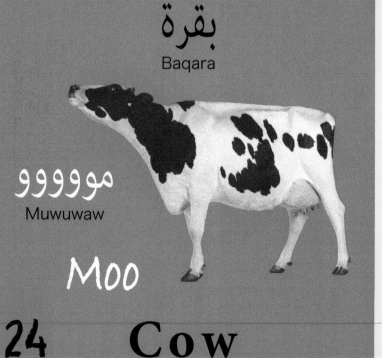

مووووو
Muwuwaw

Moo

24 # Cow

هاتف
Hatif

ترررن
Terrern

Ring

Phone

قرد
Qarad

اوووو اه
Awew ah

اوو اه
aweww ah

*Ooh-
ooh-
ahh-
ahh*

Monkey

ضفدع
Dafadae

ريبيت
Ribit

Ribbit

Frog

اصمت
Asmat

شششش
Shshshsh

Shh

Hush   25

ديك
Dik

كوكو كو
Kwkw kw

Cock-a-
doodle-doo

Rooster

طبول
Tabul

بوم بوم
Bum bum

Boom

Drums

ثعبان
Thueban

Hiss

هسسسس
Hassss

26

Snake

بومة
Bawma

هوووت
Hawawut

Hoot

Owl

نحلة طنانة
Hulat tinanatan

دززز
Dazazaz

Buzz

Bumblebee

يدين
Yudin

تصفيق
Tasfiq

Clap

Two hands

حمل
Hamal

ماااااء
Maaaaaa'

Baa

Lamb   27

يزحف
Yazahaf

Crawl

يتدحرج
Yatadaharaj

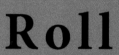

Roll

يسير
Yasir

Walk

يركض
Yarkud

Run

يثب
Ythbu

Hop

يركب
Yarkab

Ride

يقبل
Yaqbal

Kiss

يقفز
Yaqfaz

Jump 29

سعيد
Saeid

Happy

حزين
Hazin

Sad

غاضب
Ghadib

Angry

مذعور
Mazoor

Scared

محبط

Muhbat

Frustrated

متفاجئ

Mutafaji

Surprised

مصدوم

Masdum

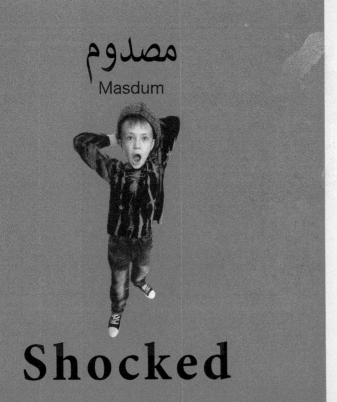

Shocked

شجاع

Shujae

Brave

31

البيسبول

Albaysbul

Baseball

كرة السلة

Kurat alsala

Basketball

التنس

Altanas

32 # Tennis

كرة القدم

Kurat alqadam

Soccer

تنس الريشة

Tans alraysha

Badminton

كرة القدم الأمريكية

Kurat alqadam al' amrikia

Football

الكرة الطائرة

Alkurat alttayira

Volleyball

جولف

Julif

Golf 33

سيارة إطفاء

Sayarat 'iitfa'

Fire truck

سيارة

Sayara

شاحنة

Shahina

34 **Car**

Truck

هليكوبتر
Hilykubtr

Helicopter

طيارة
Tiara

Airplane

قطار
Qitar

Train

قارب
Qarib

Boat   35

صغير
Smȯl

متوسط
Mtwst

كبير
Kabir

Small   Medium   Large

صغير
Smȯl

متوسط
Mtwst

كبير
Kabir

36 Small Medium   Large

كبير
Kabir

متوسط
Mtwst

صغير
Smȯl

Large   Medium   Small

كبير
Kabir

متوسط
Mtwst

صغير
Smȯl

Large   Medium   Small   37

رأس
Ras

Head

أكتاف
ʿAktaf

Shoulders

الركبتين
Alrukbatayn

38 **Knees**

اصابع القدم
ʿAsabie alqadam

Toes

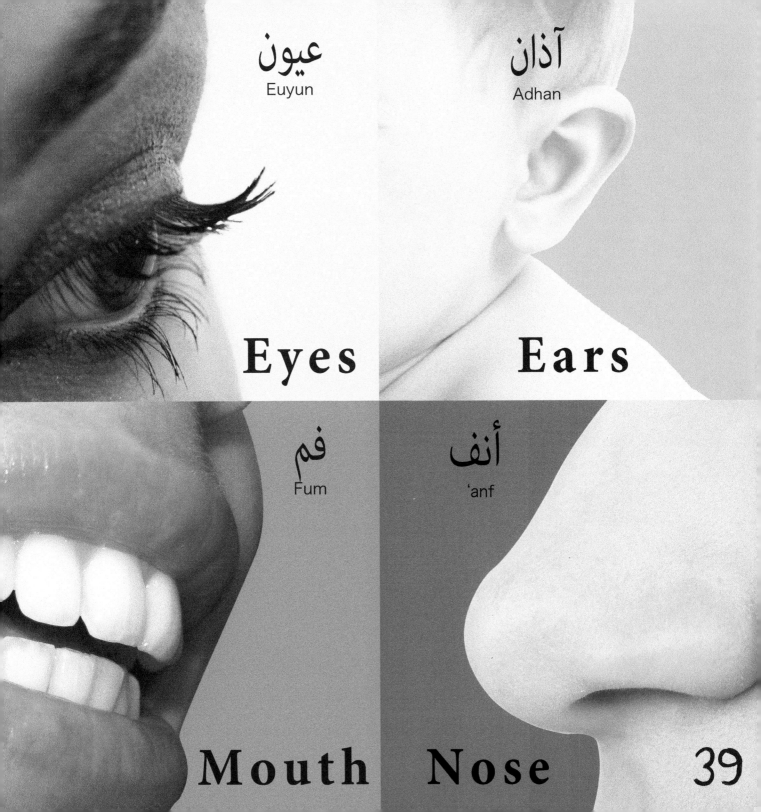

عيون
Euyun

Eyes

آذان
Adhan

Ears

فم
Fum

Mouth

أنف
'anf

Nose

39

كوب الرشف

Kub alrashf

Sippy cup

وعاء

Wiea'

Bowl

قدر

Qadar

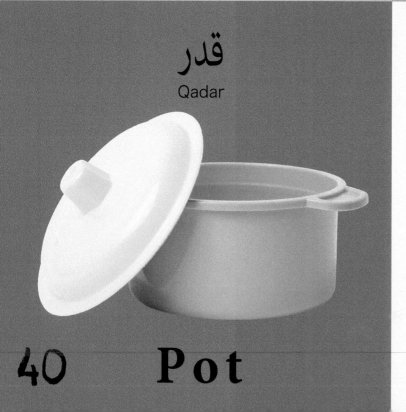

Pot

كوب

Kub

Cup

طبق
Tabaq

Plate

شوكة
Shawka

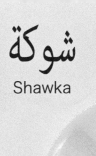

Fork

سكين
Sakin

Knife

ملعقة
Maleaqa

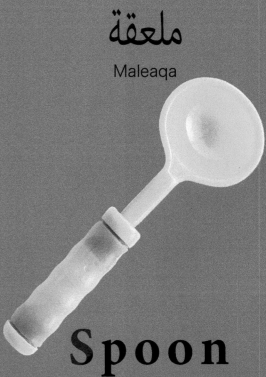

Spoon 41

قبعة
Qabea

Hat

قميص
Qamis

Shirt

بنطال
Binital

Pants

شورت
Shuirat

Shorts

قفازات

Qafazat

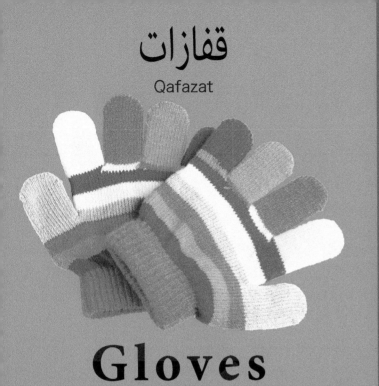

Gloves

نظارة شمسية

Nizarat shamsia

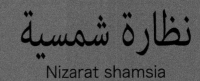

Sunglasses

جوارب

Jawarib

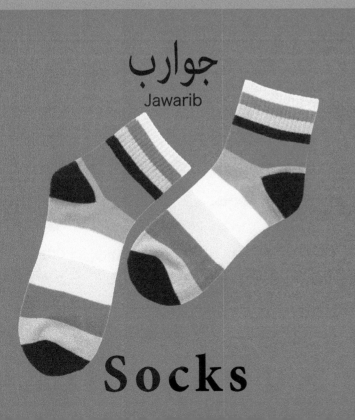

Socks

أحذية

'Ahadhiya

Shoes   43

الاستحمام
Alaistihmam

Bath time

Bath

صابون
Sabun

بطة مطاطية
Butat mutatia

44   Soap

Rubber duck

أغسل أسنانك

'Aghsal 'asnanak

Brush teeth

وقت النوم

Waqt alnuwm

Bed time

كتاب

Kitab

Book

القصرية

Alqasria

Potty

السرير

Alsarir

Bed 45

THE T♡ddLER'S handb♡♡k

Match the following to the pictures below.
Can you find **7 pumpkins**, an owl,
a rainbow, a baseball, a lion, a square,
a sad boy, a helicopter, and shoes?

وصل الكلمات الأتية بالصور: يقطين, بومة, قوس قزح
البيسبول, أسد, مربع, فتى حزين, هليكوبتر, أحذية؟

طائرة هليكوبتر
Tayirah hilikubtr

helicopter

أحذية
'Ahadhiya

shoes

البومة
Albawma

owl

البيسبول
Albaysbul

baseball

7 يقطين
7 alqare

7 pumpkins

فتى حزين
Fataan hazin

sad boy

46

أسد
'Asada

lion

مربع
Murabae

square

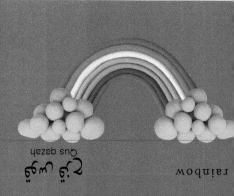

قوس قزح
Qus qazah

rainbow